PAUL JACKSON

Tricks and Games with Paper

ILLUSTRATIONS:
LOUIS SILVESTRO

ANGUS
& ROBERTSON
PUBLISHERS

Introduction

To fold a sheet of paper into a bird or frog is magic enough, but this unique book goes one step further . . . by bringing them to life! In fourteen fun projects you can learn how to fold animals and objects which flap, jump, croak, whizz, whoosh, bang, peck, snap, splat, woof, turn inside-out, lay square eggs, change pattern and change expression. Every project is brought to life by a simple yet ingenious mechanism contained within the folds. They are sure to amaze and amuse you and your friends!

The art of folding paper, or "origami" as it is more commonly known, is of ancient Japanese origin. This is the first time that many of the traditional mechanisms have been put into one volume, together with a few others invented or adapted by the author.

To fold each project, first check that you are using the correct type, shape and size of paper. If you aren't, the mechanism might not work. Next, follow the step-by-step diagrams, folding slowly and neatly as you go. Remember, the folds you are asked to make on one diagram will give you a shape which looks like the next diagram, so keep looking ahead to the next step to see what you are trying to achieve.

If, after giggling over the contents of this book, you would like to join an origami club, write to:

The Membership Secretary
British Origami Society
193 Abbey Road
Smethwick, Warley
West Midlands
England.

Membership in this society is worldwide.

If it is nearer home you may like to write to:

The New Zealand Origami
    Society
C/o Kim Hunt
79 Dunbar Road
Christchurch 3
New Zealand

In Australia there are plans to start a similar society and, if you are interested, the person to write to is:

Mr Steven Casey
1/25 Hobart Road
Murrumbeena
Victoria 3163

Symbols and Procedures

Symbols and procedures have been included at the bottom of each page.

How to make a square

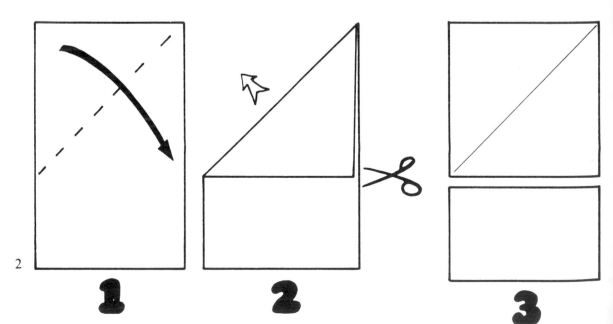

2

1   **2**   **3**

How to make a reverse fold

Banger

A paper fold unique because it makes a very loud noise! Use a rectangle of exercise book paper or typing paper, or experiment with larger sheets such as newspaper.

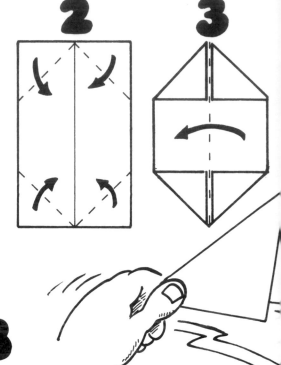

GAMES TO PLAY

Banger Shoot-out

Here's a game for two or more contestants.

Prior to a shoot-out, players each fold a Banger then unfold it. Pairs of players stand back-to-back about 1m (3ft) apart. At the starter's orders, each refolds the Banger and the first in a pair to turn and shoot his or her partner is the winner. The winners of each pair then shoot it out. Through heats and semi-finals players use their original Bangers. The finalists, however, have to fold and shoot from new pieces of paper.

fold in front	drawings become larger	hand movement	cut or tear	valley fold
fold behind	apply pressure	inflate (blow into)	repeat behind	
unfold	hold and pull	turn over		

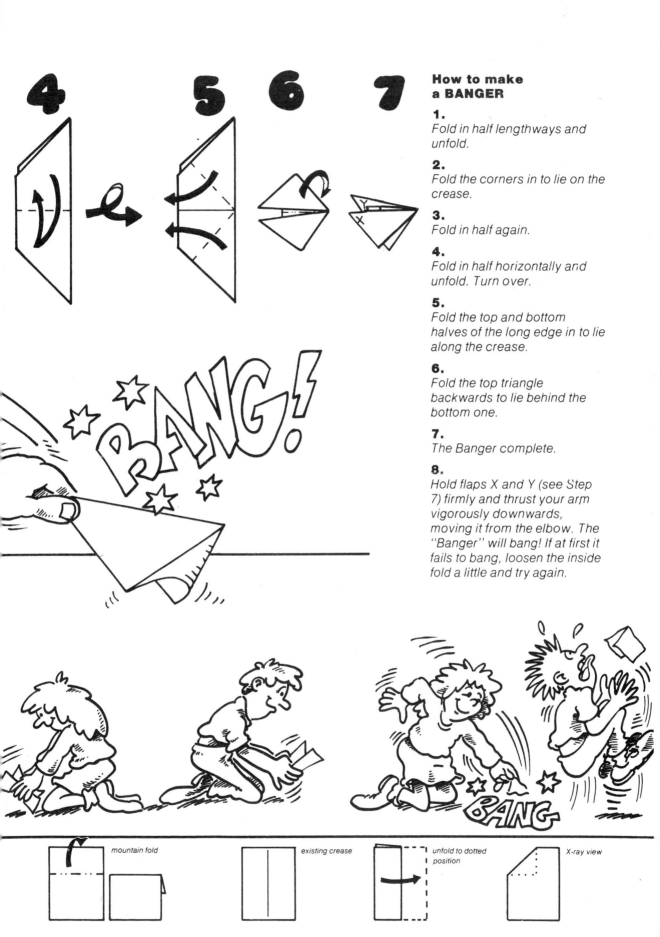

How to make a BANGER

1.
Fold in half lengthways and unfold.

2.
Fold the corners in to lie on the crease.

3.
Fold in half again.

4.
Fold in half horizontally and unfold. Turn over.

5.
Fold the top and bottom halves of the long edge in to lie along the crease.

6.
Fold the top triangle backwards to lie behind the bottom one.

7.
The Banger complete.

8.
Hold flaps X and Y (see Step 7) firmly and thrust your arm vigorously downwards, moving it from the elbow. The "Banger" will bang! If at first it fails to bang, loosen the inside fold a little and try again.

mountain fold

existing crease

unfold to dotted position

X-ray view

Happy or Sad?

This illusion will also work with heads on banknotes, which makes it a great impromptu trick to show friends. Use a piece of paper about 5–7 cm (2–3 in) square if a banknote is not to hand.

1

2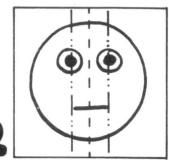

4

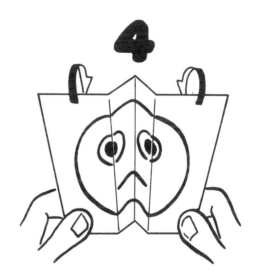

fold in front	drawings become larger	hand movement	cut or tear
fold behind	apply pressure	inflate (blow into)	valley fold
unfold	hold and pull	turn over	repeat behind

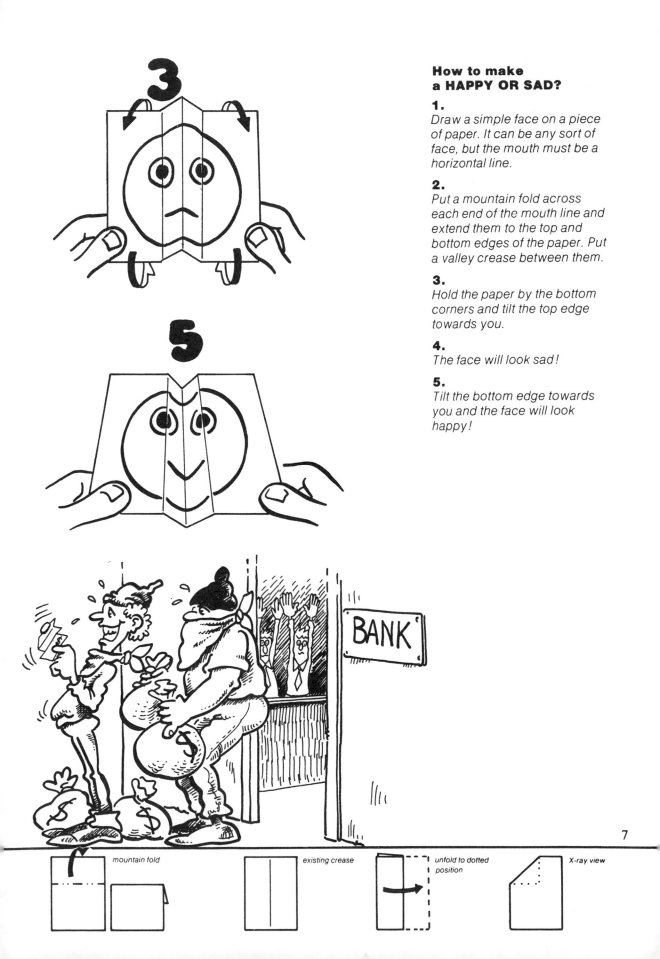

How to make a HAPPY OR SAD?

1.
Draw a simple face on a piece of paper. It can be any sort of face, but the mouth must be a horizontal line.

2.
Put a mountain fold across each end of the mouth line and extend them to the top and bottom edges of the paper. Put a valley crease between them.

3.
Hold the paper by the bottom corners and tilt the top edge towards you.

4.
The face will look sad!

5.
Tilt the bottom edge towards you and the face will look happy!

BANK

mountain fold

existing crease

unfold to dotted position

X-ray view

7

Whizzer

A remarkable mechanism, simple yet little known. Use a 16 cm by 8 cm (6 in by 3 in) rectangle of very thin paper. Airmail paper is ideal. Exercise book paper and typing paper are probably too heavy.

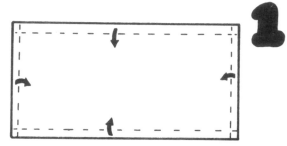

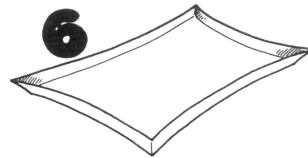

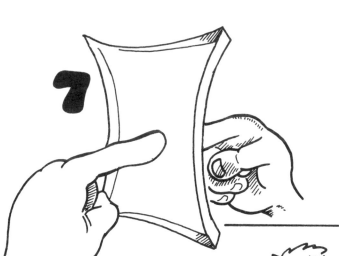

GAMES TO PLAY

Whizzer Race

Design an obstacle course which competitors must complete with a working Whizzer — racing against each other or against the clock.

8

---

fold in front	drawings become larger	hand movement	cut or tear		valley fold
fold behind	apply pressure	 inflate (blow into)			
unfold	hold and pull	 turn over	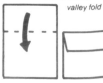 repeat behind		

How to make a WHIZZER

1.
Fold over a ½ cm (¼ in) hem along each edge.

2.
Unfold Step 1 creases.

3.
Next drawing enlarges a corner.

4.
Connect the point where the 2 creases cross with a valley fold to the corner of the paper. Repeat on the other corners.

5.
Pinch the Step 4 creases between your thumb and finger. Do it to each corner. You will have raised the edges of the paper to make a sort of shallow dish.

6.
The Whizzer complete.

7.
Hold the very middle of the Whizzer between your two first fingers. Bend your other fingers back out of the way.

8.
Stand with your arms stretched right out, elbows straight, wrists bent inwards, the "dish" facing to the left as in Step 7. Spin to your left. After a quarter of a circle, take your left first finger away from the Whizzer, which will begin to spin around on your remaining finger. Walk in a straight line or spin in a circle. Be sure to keep your finger pointing horizontally, not up, down, left or right.

9

mountain fold

existing crease

unfold to dotted position

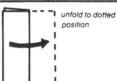
X-ray view

Inside-out Cube

A trick which seems
impossible. Even your friends
will doubt you when you
announce you can turn a cube
inside-out!

1

2

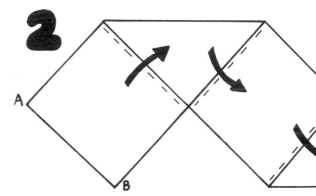

3

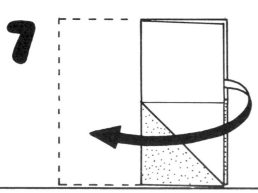

4

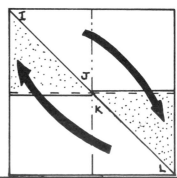

7

8

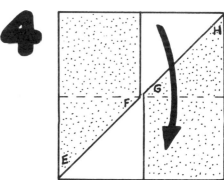

➡ fold in front	⇨ drawings become larger	✊ hand movement	✂ cut or tear	valley fold
➡ fold behind	▶ apply pressure	⟿ inflate (blow into)		
⇨ unfold	⊶ hold and pull	⟲ turn over	➡➡ repeat behind	

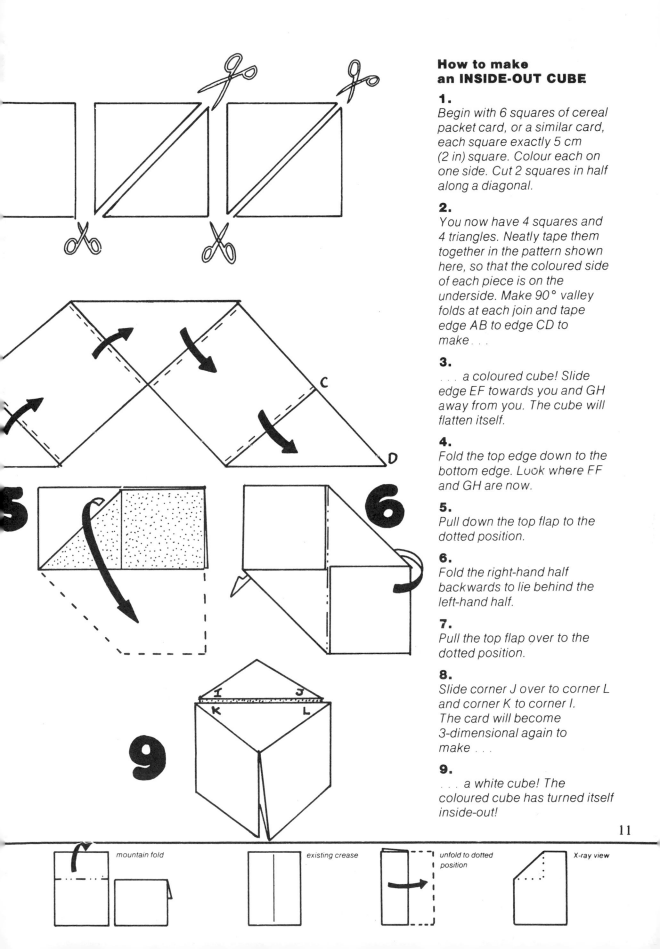

How to make an INSIDE-OUT CUBE

1.
Begin with 6 squares of cereal packet card, or a similar card, each square exactly 5 cm (2 in) square. Colour each on one side. Cut 2 squares in half along a diagonal.

2.
You now have 4 squares and 4 triangles. Neatly tape them together in the pattern shown here, so that the coloured side of each piece is on the underside. Make 90° valley folds at each join and tape edge AB to edge CD to make...

3.
... a coloured cube! Slide edge EF towards you and GH away from you. The cube will flatten itself.

4.
Fold the top edge down to the bottom edge. Look where FF and GH are now.

5.
Pull down the top flap to the dotted position.

6.
Fold the right-hand half backwards to lie behind the left-hand half.

7.
Pull the top flap over to the dotted position.

8.
Slide corner J over to corner L and corner K to corner I. The card will become 3-dimensional again to make...

9.
... a white cube! The coloured cube has turned itself inside-out!

mountain fold

existing crease

unfold to dotted position

X-ray view

Perfect Glider

There are many paper planes, but none can beat this one for grace and beauty through the air. A classic from China. Use a rectangle of thin paper about 15 cm by 20 cm (6 in by 8 in).

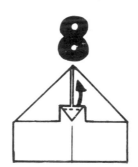

GAMES TO PLAY

Glider Skill

Two ideas to enjoy on your own or use in friendly challenge matches.

Your glider will fly with ease but how good are you at hitting a target, whether it be vertical, horizontal or moving?

How long will your glider stay aloft? Time a normal flight or try throwing your glider from a tall building.

---

fold in front	drawings become larger	hand movement	cut or tear		valley fold
fold behind	apply pressure	inflate (blow into)			
untold	hold and pull	turn over	repeat behind		

How to make a PERFECT GLIDER

1.
Fold in half lengthways and unfold. Turn the paper over so that the crease looks like a mountain fold.

2.
Fold the top corners in to lie on the crease.

3.
Fold down the top triangle.

4.
Fold the left half backwards to lie behind the right half.

5.
Tear a small square off the front and back corners at the top right.

6.
Return the rear half to the left.

7.
Fold the torn corners in to lie on the centre crease.

8.
Fold up the tab as far as it will go.

9.
Fold in half again as in Step 4.

10.
Connect the sharp corner at the top of the glider with a valley fold to the corner of the tab and continue the crease down to the bottom edge. Repeat behind.

11.
The Perfect Glider complete. To launch, hold the tab and throw horizontally with a smooth action.

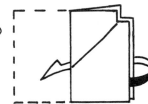

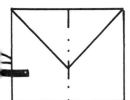

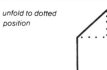

mountain fold	existing crease
unfold to dotted position	X-ray view

Snap Dragon

A rowdy favourite! Use a 15 cm (6 in) square of strong paper for best effect.

1

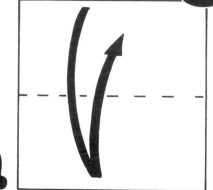

2

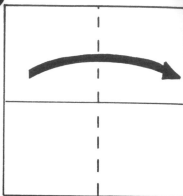

6

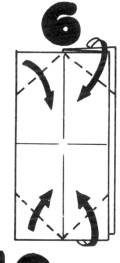

7

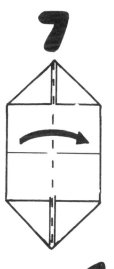

10

11

fold in front	drawings become larger	hand movement	cut or tear	valley fold
fold behind	apply pressure	inflate (blow into)		
unfold	hold and pull	 turn over	repeat behind	

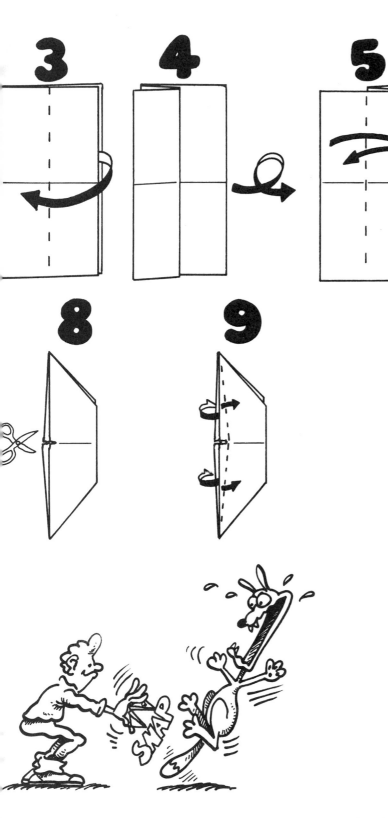

How to make a SNAP DRAGON

1.
Fold the bottom edge up to the top edge and unfold.

2.
Fold the left-hand edge over to the right-hand edge.

3.
Fold the top layer at the right over to the left-hand edge.

4.
Turn over.

5.
Fold the left-hand edge over to the right-hand edge and unfold.

6.
Fold the corners in to lie on the centre crease.

7.
Fold the left-hand edge back over to the right.

8.
Make a small tear along the horizontal crease, front and back, starting at the long vertical edge.

9.
Connect with a crease the end of each tear with the top and bottom corners.

10.
Hold as shown and "snap" the jaws together.

11.
The Snap Dragon complete. Draw fearsome eyes. If the spring in the jaws is too weak, your tears are too long.

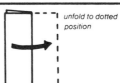

mountain fold	existing crease	unfold to dotted position	X-ray view

Jumping Frog 2

The longest recorded jump for a frog of this design is 1.78 m (6 ft 7 in). See if you can beat it! Use a small rectangle of cereal packet card or similar thin card, about 5 cm by 8 cm (2 in by 3 in).

1

2

6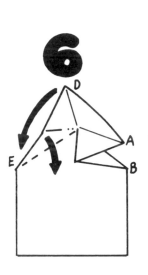

7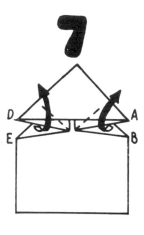

8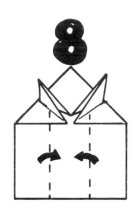

9

10

GAMES TO PLAY
Frog Olympics

Organise your own olympics with racing and jumping frogs.

Everyone enjoys the sprinting. Contestants begin simultaneously at the starter's gun and jump their frogs as many times as they can as quickly as possible towards the finishing line many yards away. First frog there wins the gold.

And you can try an obstacle race. Race your frog against others around a track littered with pitfalls — over mountains of books, up and down stairs, over soft cushions and a miniature pond made in anything handy, under a low table, between a collection of cups and basins, each waiting to trap the unlucky. The more obstacles along the way the more fun it is.

Frog jumping can also be part of the games. Frogs can be adapted to be good long jumpers or good high jumpers by folding to make the back "legs" spring mechanism shorter or longer. Experiment for the best results.

fold in front	drawings become larger	hand movement	cut or tear
fold behind	apply pressure	inflate (blow into)	
 unfold	hold and pull	turn over	repeat behind

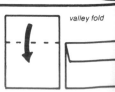 valley fold

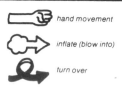

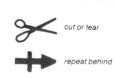

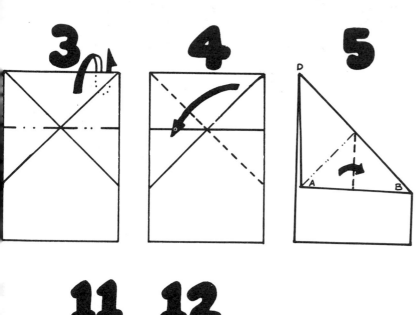

How to make a JUMPING FROG

1.
Fold the top left-hand corner over to the right-hand edge and unfold.

2.
Fold the top right-hand corner over to the left-hand edge and unfold.

3.
Make a horizontal mountain fold through the point where the creases cross and unfold.

4.
Refold Step 2.

5.
Put corner A on top of corner B, opening the pocket between A and D.

6.
Put D on top of E. The card is now symmetrical.

7.
Fold out corners A and D to the position shown in Step 8.

8.
Fold the edges in to the middle.

9.
Lightly bend the bottom edge up to the elbow. Do not make a firm crease.

10.
Lightly bend the top edge down to touch the previous bend. Do not make a firm crease.

11.
The Jumping Frog complete.

12.
Rest your finger on the frog and slide it off at the back. Your frog will jump forward.

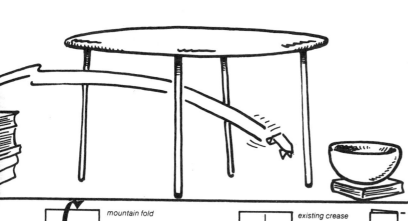

mountain fold	existing crease	unfold to dotted position	X-ray view	

Pecking Bird

A mechanism invented by the author which works best on shiny surfaces. Use a 15–20 cm (6–8 in) square of thin paper.

1
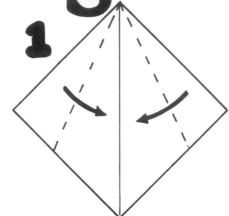

2

6
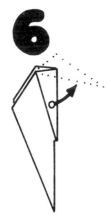

7

8

9

fold in front	drawings become larger	hand movement	cut or tear		valley fold
fold behind	apply pressure	inflate (blow into)			
unfold	hold and pull	turn over	repeat behind		

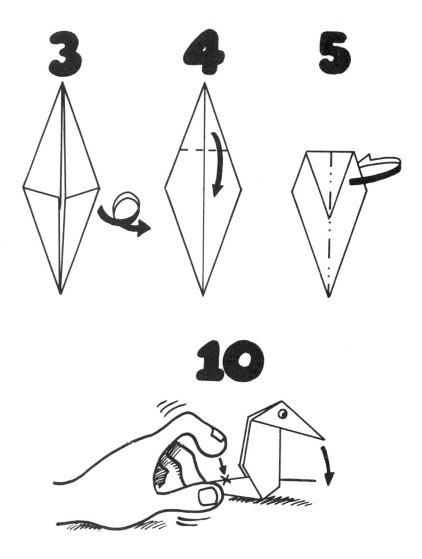

How to make a PECKING BIRD

1.
Fold in 2 adjacent edges to meet along a diagonal crease.

2.
Fold the shorter edges in to the centre crease.

3.
Turn over.

4.
Fold down the top point to the position shown in Step 5.

5.
Fold the right-hand side backwards to lie behind the left-hand side.

6.
Pull out the point to the dotted position and flatten.

7.
Valley fold the bottom point to the dotted position.

8.
Unfold Step 7.

9.
Reverse fold the bottom point between the front and back layers, along the existing crease.

10.
The Pecking Bird complete. Draw in the eyes. Hold the very tip of the reverse fold between your thumb and middle finger. Gently depress the ridge at X with your first finger and the head will bob forward to peck the ground.

mountain fold

existing crease

unfold to dotted position

X-ray view

Talking Frog

A mechanism adapted by the author from one known to French schoolchildren. Use a 15–20 cm (6–8 in) square of strong, thin paper.

1

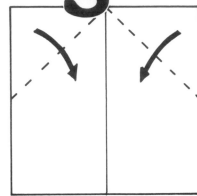

5 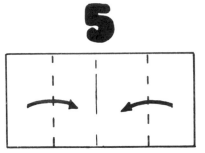 **6** 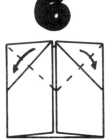 **7** 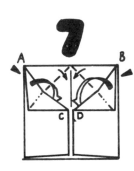 **8**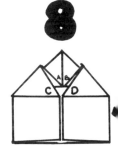

GAMES TO PLAY

Fumbling Folds?

Rather than fold this or any of the other models with two hands, form pairs where each person uses only one hand. Once you've folded a model in this way try unfolding it as well — it is just as chaotic.

For really superior fumbling you may like to try folding a model with your feet!

---

fold in front	drawings become larger	 hand movement	 cut or tear		valley fold
 fold behind	 apply pressure	inflate (blow into)	repeat behind		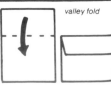
unfold	hold and pull	turn over			

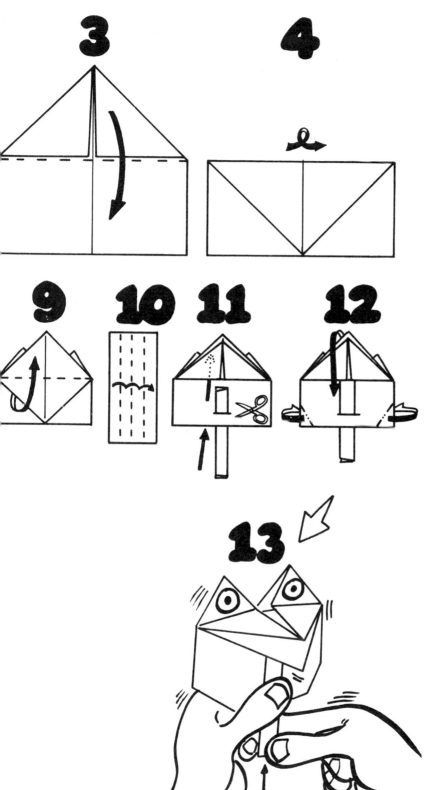

How to make a TALKING FROG

1.
Fold the left edge over to the right edge and unfold.

2.
Fold the top corners in to the crease.

3.
Fold down the top triangle.

4.
Turn over.

5.
Fold the sides in to the middle.

6.
Fold the top inside corner of each flap to the outside edge.

7.
Reverse fold A and B in to the centre crease to lie behind C and D.

8.
Turn over.

9.
Fold the bottom corner of the diamond up to the top.

10.
Fold over and over a strip of paper, which is a little longer than the height of the model.

11.
Make a small tear across the middle of the model near the bottom edge. Put the strip through the tear and push it up under the top triangle as far as it will go.

12.
Fold the bottom corners behind. Fold down the front and back triangles at the top to make the mouth come forward.

13.
The Talking Frog complete. Draw in the eyes. Hold as shown and move your right hand up and down. The frog will talk.

21

 mountain fold

 existing crease

 unfold to dotted position

 X-ray view

Kaleidoscope

Once you understand how to change the patterns described here, make your own with brightly coloured pens, or write secret messages, or draw mystery pictures, or . . . !

1

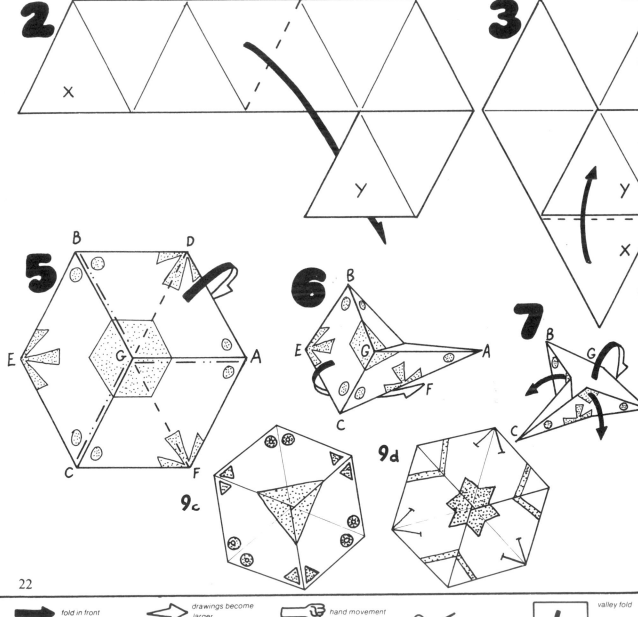

2

3

5

6

7

9c

9d

fold in front	drawings become larger	hand movement
fold behind	apply pressure	inflate (blow into)
unfold	hold and pull	turn over

cut or tear

repeat behind

valley fold

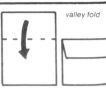

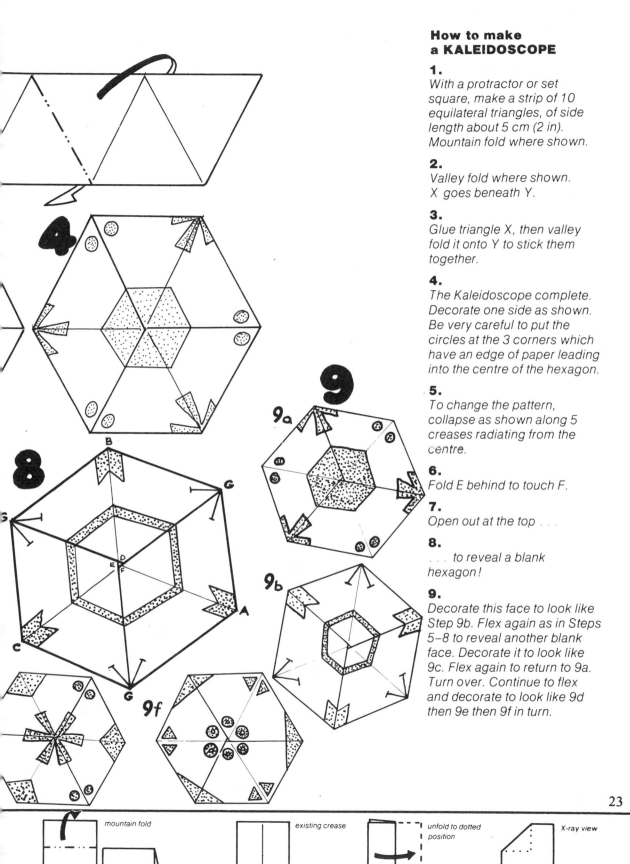

How to make a KALEIDOSCOPE

1.
With a protractor or set square, make a strip of 10 equilateral triangles, of side length about 5 cm (2 in). Mountain fold where shown.

2.
Valley fold where shown. X goes beneath Y.

3.
Glue triangle X, then valley fold it onto Y to stick them together.

4.
The Kaleidoscope complete. Decorate one side as shown. Be very careful to put the circles at the 3 corners which have an edge of paper leading into the centre of the hexagon.

5.
To change the pattern, collapse as shown along 5 creases radiating from the centre.

6.
Fold E behind to touch F.

7.
Open out at the top . . .

8.
. . . to reveal a blank hexagon!

9.
Decorate this face to look like Step 9b. Flex again as in Steps 5–8 to reveal another blank face. Decorate it to look like 9c. Flex again to return to 9a. Turn over. Continue to flex and decorate to look like 9d then 9e then 9f in turn.

23

mountain fold existing crease unfold to dotted position X-ray view

Barking Dog

A mechanism invented by the author. Practise barking noises to accompany the action! Use a 15–20 cm (6–8 in) square of strong, thin paper.

1

2

3

7

8

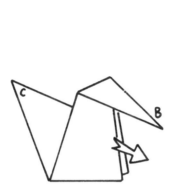

9

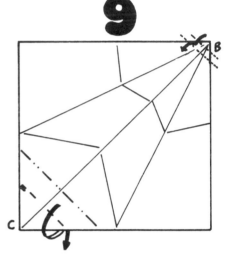

12

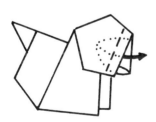

13

fold in front	drawings become larger	hand movement	cut or tear
fold behind	apply pressure	inflate (blow into)	valley fold
unfold	hold and pull	turn over	repeat behind

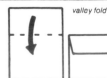

How to make a BARKING DOG

1.
Fold in half along a diagonal.

2.
Fold the top edge of the front layer to the crease and unfold.

3.
Fold the bottom corner to the dotted position and unfold. This crease and the Step 2 crease meet at A.

4.
Reverse fold along the Step 3 crease.

5.
Refold Step 2.

6.
Mountain fold the rear flap to match Step 5.

7.
Valley fold the top point to the position shown in Step 8.

8.
Unfold all the creases!

9.
Fold the tip of corner B (see Step 8) over and over. Make parallel mountain and valley folds across corner C to create a pleat.

10.
Recrease as shown. Look carefully — some valleys are changed to mountains! Collapse the paper, forming all the creases at the same time as you go, to create a shape which looks like Step 11.

11.
Reverse fold the nose inside the head, but first make a valley fold to locate the position of the crease (see "Symbols and Procedures").

12.
Pull the nose back out along another reverse fold.

13.
The Barking Dog complete. Hold as shown and pull the tail to make the head bark!

25

mountain fold	existing crease	unfold to dotted position	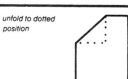 X-ray view

Waterbomb

An old favourite, yet few seem to know how to lock it together properly. Use a 15–20 cm (6–8 in) square of strong paper.

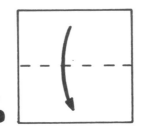

1

2

6

7

8

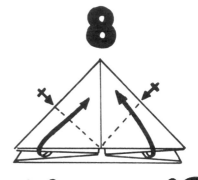

11

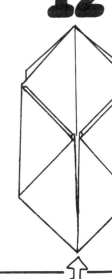

12

9

10

GAMES TO PLAY
Large-scale Fun

It would probably require a team of four to make this model from a 2m (7ft) square, but it has been done. There could be difficulty in inflating the model and filling it, but imagine the chaos a bomb this size could cause!

26

fold in front	drawings become larger		hand movement		valley fold
fold behind	▶ apply pressure	 inflate (blow into)		✂ cut or tear	
unfold	⊸ hold and pull	♀ turn over		repeat behind	

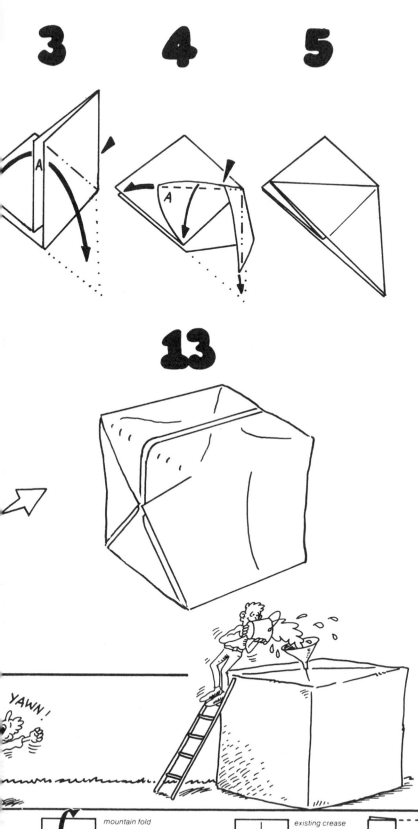

How to make a WATERBOMB

1.
Fold the top edge down to the bottom edge.

2.
Fold the right-hand edge over to the left-hand edge and unfold slightly to look like Step 3.

3.
Apply pressure on the vertical crease to separate the layers of paper and open pocket A.

4.
Pocket A opening. Squash it flat . . .

5.
. . . to make a big triangle. Turn over.

6.
Lift up both layers of the big square.

7.
Apply pressure as in Step 3 to open pocket B. Squash flat to make another big triangle.

8.
On the front triangle only, fold the sharp corners up to the blunter corner. Turn over and repeat behind.

9.
Fold the left and right corners of the front diamond in to the centre. Repeat behind.

10.
Fold the loose sharp corners also in to the middle. Repeat behind.

11.
Valley fold C and D into the pockets. Repeat behind.

12.
Blow into the hole at the bottom to inflate the paper. If the hole is too small, loosen the creases at Step 8.

13.
The Waterbomb complete — once you've filled it with water!

27

mountain fold	existing crease	unfold to dotted position	X-ray view

Laying a Square

An unusual and surprising mechanism. Practise clucking noises to accompany the action! Use a 15–20 cm (6–8 in) square of strong, thin paper.

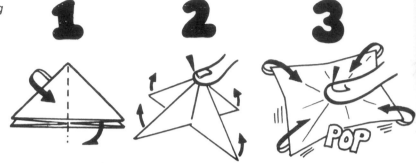

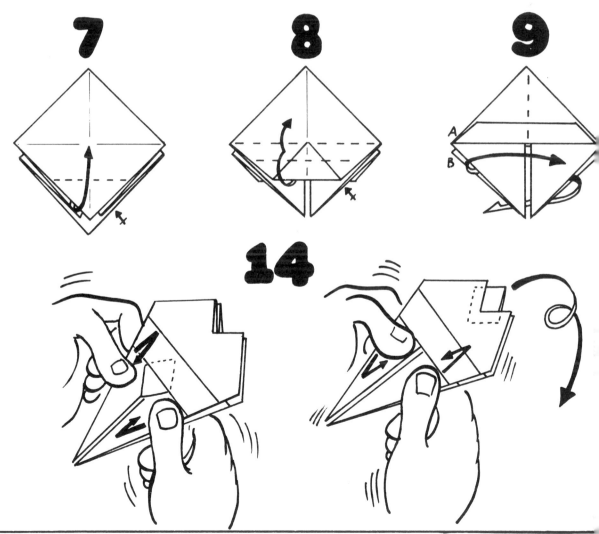

⇒ fold in front	⇨ drawings become larger	🖐 hand movement	✂ cut or tear	valley fold
⇒ fold behind	▸ apply pressure	🗯 inflate (blow into)		
⇨ unfold	⌾→ hold and pull	☊ turn over	⊹→ repeat behind	

Egg

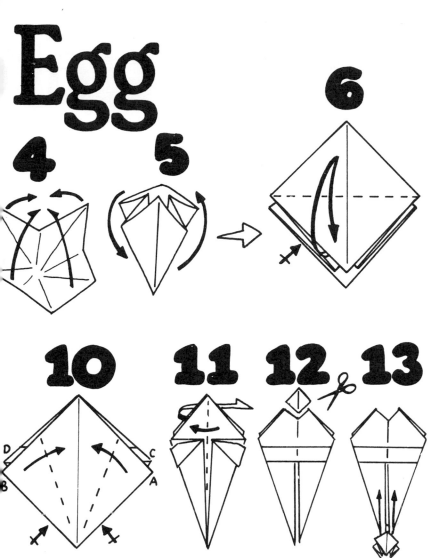

How to make LAYING A SQUARE EGG

1.
Begin with Step 8 of the "Waterbomb". Fan out the 4 flaps to make a star.

2.
Press down on the middle . . .

3.
. . . until the square is almost flat, when it will suddenly pop inside out.

4.
Bring the 4 corners together at the top.

5.
Turn upside down and flatten.

6.
Fold the top layer at the bottom corner to the top corner and unfold. Repeat behind.

7.
Fold the top layer in to the middle. Repeat behind.

8.
Fold over and over. Repeat behind.

9.
Valley fold A to lie on C. Mountain fold D to lie behind B.

10.
Fold the bottom edges of the diamond in to the centre crease. Repeat behind.

11.
Unfold Step 9.

12.
Carefully cut a square (the "egg") off the top corner.

13.
Put the "legs" in between the front and back layers of the egg and slide the egg up to the position in Step 14.

14.
Hold as shown. Vigorously rub the legs up and down against each other. The egg will slide up out of sight. Keep rubbing and it will soon fall out of the top. You have laid a Square Egg!

mountain fold	existing crease	unfold to dotted position	X-ray view

Flapping Bird

Thought by knowledgeable paper folders to be the greatest origami mechanism. Use a 15–20 cm (6–8 in) square of strong, thin paper.

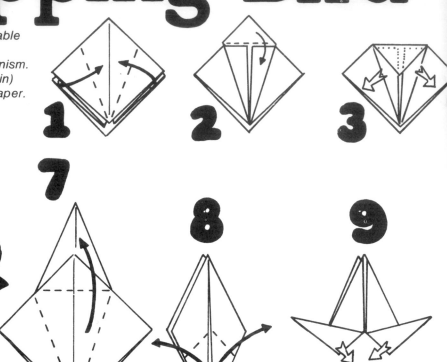

1

2

3

6

7

8

9

GAMES TO PLAY
Minute Models

There is a world record for the smallest model Flapping Bird, set by a Japanese paper folder. His model, which would have been folded with the aid of pins and a magnifying glass, was made from a square with sides of just 2.9 mm ($\frac{1}{10}$ in).

How small can you go with this and some of the other models in this book?

 fold in front

 fold behind

 unfold

 drawings become larger

 apply pressure

 hold and pull

hand movement

inflate (blow into)

 turn over

 cut or tear

 repeat behind

 valley fold

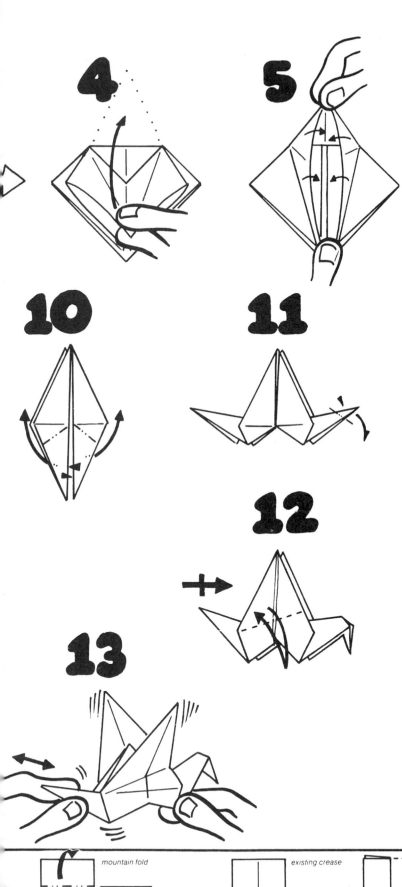

How to make a FLAPPING BIRD

1.
Begin at Step 6 of "Laying a Square Egg". Top flaps only, fold the bottom edges of the diamond in to the centre crease.

2.
Fold down the top triangle.

3.
Unfold Step 1.

4.
Hold the single-layer bottom tip of the diamond and pull it upwards towards the dotted position.

5.
Collapse flat.

6.
Turn over.

7.
Repeat Steps 1–6.

8.
Valley fold the bottom points out to the position shown in Step 9.

9.
Unfold Step 8.

10.
Reverse fold along Step 9 creases.

11.
Reverse fold the head.

12.
Fold the nearside wing forward and unfold. Turn over and repeat behind.

13.
The Flapping Bird complete. Hold the neck and pull the tail to and fro to make the wings flap.

| | mountain fold | | existing crease | | unfold to dotted position | | X-ray view |

ANGUS & ROBERTSON PUBLISHERS

*Unit 4, Eden Park, 31 Waterloo Road,
North Ryde, NSW, Australia 2113
and
16 Golden Square, London W1R 4BN,
United Kingdom*

*First published in Australia by
Angus & Robertson Publishers in 1985
First published in the United Kingdom
by Angus & Robertson (UK) Ltd in 1985*

*Reprinted 1985 (three times),
1986 (three times), 1987 (three times),
1988, 1989*

Copyright © Paul Jackson 1985

*National Library of Australia
Cataloguing-in-publication data.*

*Jackson, Paul, 1956-
    Tricks and games with paper.*

ISBN 0 207 15038 9.

1. Origami - Juvenile literature. 1. Title.

736'.982

*Typeset in Helvetica by
G & L Typesetters*

*Printed in Great Britain by
Scotprint Ltd, Musselburgh, Scotland*